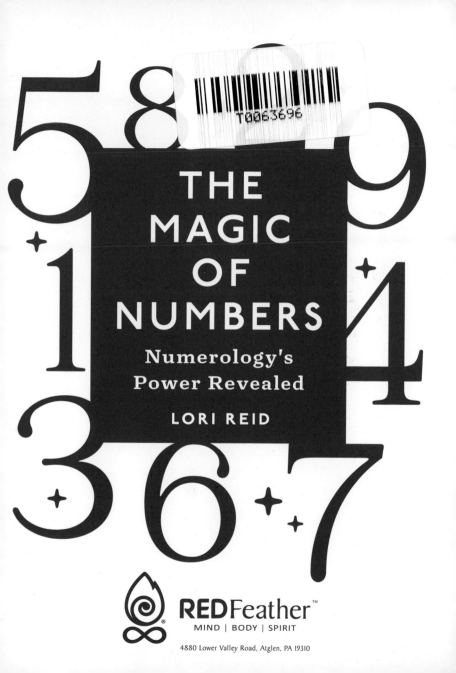

THE
MAGIC
OF
NUMBERS

Numerology's
Power Revealed

LORI REID

REDFeather™

MIND | BODY | SPIRIT

4880 Lower Valley Road, Atglen, PA 19310

Other REDFeather Titles by the Author:
Your Health in Your Hands: Hand Reading as a Guide to Well-Being, ISBN 978-0-7643-5885-2

Other REDFeather Titles on Related Subjects:
Numerology and the Divine Triangle, Dusty Bunker, ISBN 978-0-7643-6203-3

Numerology and Your Future, 2nd Edition: The Predictive Power of Numbers, Dusty Bunker, ISBN 978-0-7643-6035-0

The Numbers of Your Life: Numerology & Personal Discovery, Maiya Gray-Cobb, ISBN 978-0-7643-4142-7

Cover design by Ashley Millhouse
Type set in Turnip/P22 Underground/Garamond

Please note that all names used as examples in this book are fictitious.

ISBN: 978-0-7643-6530-0
Printed in India

Published by REDFeather Mind, Body, Spirit
An imprint of Schiffer Publishing, Ltd.
4880 Lower Valley Road
Atglen, PA 19310
Phone: (610) 593-1777; Fax: (610) 593-2002
Email: Info@redfeathermbs.com
Web: www.redfeathermbs.com

For our complete selection of fine books on this and related subjects, please visit our website at www.redfeathermbs.com. You may also write for a free catalog.

REDFeather Mind, Body, Spirit's titles are available at special discounts for bulk purchases for sales promotions or premiums. Special editions, including personalized covers, corporate imprints, and excerpts, can be created in large quantities for special needs. For more information, contact the publisher.

We are always looking for people to write books on new and related subjects. If you have an idea for a book, please contact us at proposals@schifferbooks.com.

CONTENTS

INTRODUCTION
4

1
BIRTHDAYS
6

2
WHAT'S IN A NAME?
18

3
LOVE AND ATTRACTION
30

4
WORK AND MONEY
52

5
KEY TO THE DOOR
64

CONCLUSION: A WORLD OF WONDER
78

INTRODUCTION

Numerology—the study of numbers—is an ancient science. There are no records of when and how it came into being, but we can be fairly confident that numbers have probably been studied by just about every civilization since the beginning of time. We know from historical records that numerology was practiced by the ancient Chinese, the Egyptians, the Hebrews, the Greeks, the Arabians, and the Romans. Pythagoras was one of its greatest exponents, and it is from his theories and teachings, handed down from pupil to pupil, that we have been able to gain much of our understanding of the subject today.

Perhaps what Pythagoras, and sometime after him Agrippa, has taught us is that numbers can be looked at on a variety of levels, some fairly simple and others intricately complex. On the one hand there is the purely logical and linear mathematical calculation—the adding and subtracting as in schoolroom sums. On the other, there is the more esoteric element to numbers, that side of the study that describes time and space and the very essence of nature itself.

It is almost as if the ancients recognized a primal mathematical formula in all matter and form, a geometric pattern that influences and governs all living things. Thus, it was believed that numbers provided the key to the mysteries of the universe. And so it was that number systems over the centuries were developed to crack the code, and, slowly, as numerology evolved into a complex language of its

own, it became recognized and firmly established both for divinatory purposes and as a means of character analysis.

Essentially, numerology is based on the principle that numbers correspond to particular forces in nature. Each number, it is believed, emits a pulse, a vibration that resonates differently from every other number, each one producing a particular numerical magnetism. It is this innate vibration that works on all matter, setting up patterns of corelationships, of causes and effects. By understanding these patterns, we too can get a glimpse of how to crack the code.

Thus, times and dates, being number calculations, all hold an esoteric significance that not only have an integral meaning of their own but also interconnect and correspond to times, events, people, and places in the present, in the past, and in the future too. In just the same way, by giving letters of the alphabet a numerical equivalent, it is possible to convert any name into a number, which then gives us an understanding of its quintessential character, meaning, and significance.

Depending on the different levels of interpretation, numerology can be as easy or as complex as the practitioner might want to make it, yet every level yields no less a fascinating picture and understanding of our universe as any other. Simply put, the system is based on the use of the nine primary numbers, each of which symbolizes a basic set of principles. Each number, then, describes a group of archetypal features and paints a picture in shorthand form of the fundamental forces that underlie existence. The number 2, for example, represents the dual, changeable, reflective aspects of nature, while the number 8 symbolizes wealth and good fortune, and the number 9 describes humanitarianism, spirituality, and the higher idealistic aspirations.

By using numerology, then, our names, our dates of birth, and even the number of the house in which we live will reveal a new meaning, a new understanding of the forces of nature that permeate and govern our lives.

CHAPTER
ONE

BIRTHDAYS

CONSIDER HOW OFTEN

in the course of your life you have to write your date of birth. Filling in job application forms; getting a driver's license; giving your bank details; applying for life insurance, a passport, or a credit card; at the doctor's and the dentist's—in fact, on practically every official document or in any transaction you can think of. And yet, as you blithely write down those figures, so special and so personal to you, little do you realize the significance and potency that lies within them.

Indeed, numerologists say that your destiny, and all those funny little quirks of fate that occur in your life, are linked to the very numbers that make up your date of birth.

The fundamental principle behind numerology is that every number contains a unique vibrational influence that has a direct effect on matter and on all living things. So your date of birth, then, will give a great deal of information about your life—your drive, your motivation, your expectations, your dreams and ambitions, how you work, and what makes you tick.

Additionally, numbers occur in cycles, and, just to send your mind in a spin for a minute, they often occur in cycles within cycles! But the critical importance about your actual date of birth is that this number will reveal insights into your life cycle and into the sequences of events that are likely to occur to you throughout your life.

You will already have noticed that there have been periods in your life of hectic activity followed by periods of comparative peace and quiet. There will have been times when you were brimming with inspiration and good ideas. At other times your mind might have seemed quite stagnant, and life itself may have appeared dull and uneventful. Lucky opportunities perhaps have come your way with amazing regularity, and then misfortune may have struck repeated blows so that you felt, for a time, that your very footsteps were dogged by bad luck.

You may also have noticed that certain numbers tend to recur in your life. Consider why you have a lucky number at all, and then ask yourself how you realized that that particular number *was* lucky for you in the first place. Perhaps originally it was the winning number of a raffle ticket that you bought by chance. It won once, so next time you asked for that number again. And if it wins a second time for you, you know you're onto a good thing.

Perhaps it is that you've noticed that events turn out favorably for you on a certain date, so when that comes around, you put your best efforts into it, ask for a raise, arrange a job interview or important meeting, sign agreements, or target a new project to start on that very day. And when these things are more or less successful, they reinforce the notion that that is indeed an especially lucky date for you, and one in which, in the future, you should project your best efforts. Similarly, you will come to realize that there are certain dates in which you are best advised to keep a low profile, since here fortune is not on your side, and the vibrational influences are not in your favor.

With a little knowledge of the principles behind numerology, you will be able to get a good idea of how numbers influence your life and how you are governed by the numerical cycle that is at the fundamental core of existence. And by understanding that, you will be able to turn to your advantage those numbers that are favorable to you. It all begins with your date of birth.

DESTINY NUMBERS

When added together and reduced to a single digit, your date of birth will reveal what numerology calls your Life or Destiny Number. This number, you will find, is the one that rules your life and the one that has a habit of cropping up time and again for you with uncanny regularity.

At this level, only the primary numbers of 1 to 9 are used, so that all birthdays have to be reduced to a single digit. So, to convert your date of birth, you simply add together the day, month, and year when you were born. The months are converted into their numerical equivalence according to their sequence in the year, so that January is 1, February is 2, March is 3, and so on to December, which, of course is 12.

Having added them together, you will undoubtedly arrive at a four-figure number. Now, because you will be working on the 1–9 system, this large figure has to be further reduced until a primary number is arrived at, so here you just add each digit of that compound number together, and if this produces another double figure, add those two together, and so on until you are left with a single unit. In fact, by continual addition, every number, no matter how large, can be reduced to one single primary number. So, let us take as an example someone who was born on March 1, 1995:

Example

Day	1
Month: March = 3	3
Year	1995
	——
Total	1999

Now reduce 1999 to a single digit thus: $1 + 9 + 9 + 9 = 28$
next, add the 2 and 8 together: $2 + 8 = 10$
then reduce finally: $1 + 0 = 1$

So the numerical value, or Destiny Number, of being born on March 1, 1995, is ONE.

When you have converted your date of birth, check the following qualities that are associated with your own personal Destiny Number. This will be the number of greatest significance in your life and the one you will find likely to recur in your day-to-day affairs. But make a note, too, of the numbers that vibrate harmoniously with it, because these will have a positive relationship with your own Destiny Number and so are likely to be favorable to you as well.

The Key Words for each Destiny Number will give you a brief outline of your positive characteristics, and the Negative Qualities will show you the areas that perhaps could do with improvement. Also listed are the anatomical parts of the body considered to be associated with that number, together with other influences such as color and the day of the week that is lucky for you. But equally important information at this stage is about achieving your potential in life according to your personal number, which you will find in the list headed "Directions."

DESTINY NUMBER 1

Keywords: Willpower, purpose, daring, single-mindedness, assertiveness, leadership, courage, love.

Significance: Number ONE is a positive number. Being the first digit, it conveys a sense of leadership and originality.

Negative Qualities: Arrogance is the major pitfall of this number. Because it has the connotation of single-mindedness, ONE can become egocentric, selfishly blind to the needs of others, self-centered and inconsiderate in its pursuit of its own independence, and race to become the first, the biggest, and the best.

Directions: It is either through physical activity, such as in sports, or through the active use of creative ideas that those with a ONE Destiny Number will succeed in life.

Anatomical Links: Relates to the head, face, hair, and lungs.

Color Associations: Red

Vibrates with: 1, 4, and 7

Uneasy with: 6

Planetary Influence: The Sun

Lucky Day: Sunday

DESTINY NUMBER 2

Keywords: Balance, cooperation, constructivity, considerateness, placidity, receptivity.

Significance: The number TWO is both positive and negative. It is the number of opposites, of contrast, of duality. It is a passive number, always coming down on the side of justice, striving to attain harmony and balance in life.

Negative Qualities: The dual nature of this number can produce a lack of self-confidence and thus lead to indecision and a good deal of sitting on the fence. The negative side of TWO, therefore, symbolizes a refusal to accept responsibility and an inability to make definitive decisions.

Directions: Best achievements for TWO Destiny Numbers come through teamwork and tasks involving group decision-making.

Anatomical Links: Relates to the brain, the solar plexus, and the nervous system.

Color Associations: Cream

Vibrates with: 2, 7, 8, and 4

Uneasy with: 5

Planetary Influence: The Moon

Lucky Day: Monday

DESTINY NUMBER 3

Keywords: Energy, self-expression, intellect, wit, persuasiveness, charm, success, versatility.

Significance: THREE is the sign of the Trinity and is symbolized by the triangle. Psychologically, it represents sociability and the healing professions. Its forte lies in diversification of interests and the connection with people and the public at large.

Negative Qualities: Jealousy, superficiality, and impatience are the major downfalls of the number THREE. It is a changeable, mutual number, with so many strings to its bow that it can become inconsistent, scattering its energies and depleting its resources.

Directions: Success may be achieved by THREE Destiny Numbers through their heightened creative talents in conjunction with their excellent social skills.

Anatomical Links: Number THREE corresponds to language, so it will relate to the organs of speech, which include the tongue, throat, and voice box.

Color Associations: Yellow

Vibrates with: 3, 6, and 9

Uneasy with: 4 and 8

Planetary Influence: Mercury

Lucky Day: Tuesday

DESTINY NUMBER 4

Keywords: Practicality, self-control, steadfastness, conscientiousness, faithfulness.

Significance: FOUR is the sign of the square, and, as such, it is a solid, stable number. In nature it is seen to recur in the four seasons; the four elements of Earth, Air, Fire, and Water; and in the four points of the compass. Thus, a sense of order and routine is associated with FOUR. Psychologically, it is the number of the builder, of practical construction, dependable and hardworking, solid as a rock.

Negative Qualities: The solid stability and steadfastness of this number can turn into a negative, stubborn, plodding, dyed-in-the-wool attitude toward life.

Directions: Steady work that prides itself on its thoroughness and good, solid common sense is the way FOUR Destiny Numbers will climb the ladder to success.

Anatomical Links: Relates to the stomach.

Color Associations: Green

Vibrates with: 4, 1, 7, and 8

Uneasy with: 5

Planetary Influence: Uranus

Lucky Day: Saturday

DESTINY NUMBER 5

Keywords: Adventure, aspiration, freedom, belief, change, versatility, sensuality, sexuality, lasciviousness.

Significance: FIVE is the number of the pentangle, the five-pointed star believed to possess magical powers and thus used as a mystical symbol. It is associated with gregariousness, adaptability, and versatility and is the mark of the quick-witted thinker. It is highly appropriate that FIVE is the number of the senses because more than anything else, this digit is associated with self-indulgence. It is the number that rules the physical pleasures in life: eating, drinking, recreation, having sex. Indeed, everything that has to do with fertility and procreation is linked with the number FIVE.

Negative Qualities: The negative side of the number FIVE is selfishness, instability, irresponsibility, overindulgence, and a lack of self-discipline. The sensuality associated with this digit can all too easily turn into decadence and, in extreme cases, into corruption.

Directions: For the FIVE Destiny Number, success may come through entrepreneurial projects and schemes. Those who are less business-minded may find that life as a traveler or explorer satisfies their ambitions.

Anatomical Links: FIVE relates to the liver and the gall bladder.

Color Associations: Blue

Vibrates with: 5 and 3

Uneasy with: 4

Planetary Influence: Mercury

Lucky Day: Thursday

DESTINY NUMBER 6

Keywords: Responsibility, dependability, integration, family orientation, kindness, sympathy, service to others.

Significance: SIX is the hexagon sometimes formed by intertwining two equilateral triangles. It is a homely number, representing domesticity, reliability, and responsibility. It is the number associated with healing and with the welfare of the nation. Idealism, honesty, and harmony are the principles governing the number SIX.

Negative Qualities: Obstinacy is perhaps the most negative quality. Other adverse factors are a sense of overprotection and an instinct to meddle in other people's affairs.

Directions: Destiny Number SIX often succeeds in vocational work. People with this number have the potential to achieve a high degree of respect from their colleagues and could well climb to a lofty position in the community. The phrase "a pillar of society" fits this number well.

Anatomical Links: SIX relates to the circulatory system, to the heart and the blood stream.

Color Associations: Indigo

Vibrates with: 6, 3, and 9

Uneasy with: 1 and 8

Planetary Influence: Venus

Lucky Day: Friday

DESTINY NUMBER 7

Keywords: Introspection, intellect, sensitivity, philosophy, discernment, solitariness.

Significance: SEVEN is regarded as a complete or perfect number, divisible by no other number than by itself and 1. Biblically, the period of Creation was said to have taken place over seven days, and of course there are seven days in a week. Celestially, seven stars make up the Pleiades, and seven notes make up the music of the spheres, while historically we have seven Wonders of the World. As a vibratory number, SEVEN is associated with wisdom and the pursuit of knowledge. Sophisticated, cultured, and refined, SEVEN is imbued with a mystical, mysterious quality and takes a lofty view of life.

Negative Qualities: Secretive and solitary, its haughty attitude can turn into condescension and sarcasm leveled at anything or anyone considered inferior.

Directions: Intellectual thought, philosophy, and scientific research bring fulfillment and achievement. Destiny number SEVEN individuals find satisfaction delving into the realms of the mystique, occult, or complementary or alternative studies.

Anatomical Links: SEVEN relates to the spleen.

Color Associations: Violet

Vibrates with: 7, 1, 2, and 4

Uneasy with: 9

Planetary Influence: Neptune

Lucky Day: Wednesday

DESTINY NUMBER 8

Keywords: Materialism, wealth, power, success, influence, understanding, practicality, ambition, organizational flair.

Significance: Oriental philosophy considers the number EIGHT as the luckiest number of all. Indeed, symbolically it is associated with prosperity and worldly success. Cool and calculative in outlook, EIGHT is the number of big business, of commerce, of ambition, of executives, and of wealth creation.

Negative Qualities: An unscrupulous pursuit of ambition and the drive for recognition and material gain give this number its negative image of impatience, intolerance, and power-grabbing insensitivity.

Directions: Naturally born with the Midas touch, honesty is paramount for the Destiny Number EIGHT to enjoy happy wealth and success. Machiavellian tactics and dishonesty can, with this number, lead to disfavor and financial problems.

Anatomical Links: EIGHT rules the eyes and lower intestines.

Color Associations: Ivory white

Vibrates with: 8, 2, and 4

Uneasy with: 3 and 6

Planetary Influence: Saturn

Lucky Day: Saturday

DESTINY NUMBER 9

Keywords: Humanitarianism, philanthropy, compassion, understanding, idealism, romance.

Significance: NINE is associated with high principles. It is the number of the philosopher, high-minded and broad-thinking. Idealistic and romantic, it governs humanitarian concerns. Sympathy, empathy, and goodwill toward others come under the auspices of the number NINE.

Negative Qualities: "Jack of all trades and master of none" may be applied to the number NINE. Impulsiveness, lack of self-discipline, and a tendency to become distracted and to easily lose concentration are drawbacks here.

Directions: Philanthropic gestures and humanitarian pursuits are more likely to see money flow out rather than flow in. But material prosperity is not essentially what makes Destiny Number NINE happy or fulfilled. Success here stems from the satisfaction derived from service given to others and from the good cheer this spreads to the community.

Anatomical Links: NINE rules the sexual organs and urinary system.

Color Associations: Crimson

Vibrates with: 9, 3, and 6

Uneasy with: 7

Planetary Influence: Mars

Lucky Day: Thursday

Having calculated your Destiny Number and having built a profile of yourself and of your potential, you can start to use the Magic of Numbers to your advantage. Experiment by scheduling important appointments on favorable days. If you are a SIX, for example, choose the 6th day of the month in which to begin a new project or on which to sign an agreement. Or at least a day that adds up to SIX—the 15th or 24th, let's say. And perhaps your best efforts or new plans could be put into operation in June, the 6th month of the year.

As an exercise, write out a list of important events that have occurred to you, beginning with your date of birth. Against each entry, remember to convert the dates into a primary number. The sort of events to jot down might include, for example, moving to a new house, leaving school, going to college, landing a great job, falling in love, suffering the loss of a significant person, enjoying a fabulous holiday, giving birth to a baby, or winning the lottery.

Now, check over these dates—or Destiny Numbers—that mark important events in your life. How often do they recur? Or perhaps it is the interval of years between such major events that may be of significance. Playing with numbers in this way can be a revelation.

Many famous people throughout history have discovered the power of their Destiny Numbers and used it to their advantage. Among them is the much-cited businessman W. K. Kellogg, whose Destiny Number was SEVEN. He insisted on signing all important documents on the 7th of the month and finalizing deals either in July (7th month) or on a date that reduced to 7. We will never know whether it was his shrewd business mind or his clever manipulations of his Destiny Number that contributed to his success. Perhaps it was a combination of both. Whichever, W. K. Kellogg amassed an empire worth millions.

So, having calculated the numerical equivalent of your date of birth, the next step is to work out your Expression Number. The Expression Number is resonated through your name. When the Destiny Number vibrates harmoniously with the Expression Number, life is found to be a smoother affair, with life targets and achievements more easily met. Not all is lost, however, if the two numbers are discordant, because, while of course one's birth or Destiny Number is fixed in history, a name can be changed. Shortening a Christian name, using a nickname, or, as so many superstar celebrities do, adopting a different name altogether will not only alter one's personal image but will also change the vibrational influence that the new name gives out. Changing your name could change the whole course of your life!

CHAPTER TWO

WHAT'S IN A NAME?

THE NAME YOU WERE

given at birth is more than a mere label that distinguishes you from the next person. Your name reveals a great deal about you. It can give clues about your nationality, ancestry, status, and position. It can reveal your parents' tastes, inclinations, and political persuasions; with a few exceptions it can refer to your gender, and, because fashions for names vary from generation to generation, it can also hint at your age.

Your name is your *brand*, which, even before you enter the room, has already painted a picture of you in other people's minds.

Whether in reality you live up to that image—either physically or psychologically, be it in your own eyes or in other people's—is an interesting matter and gives rise to several questions. For example, is it pure luck or chance that a certain name suits a certain individual? Is it that we grow to "fit" our names, as it were? Or perhaps it has to do with other people's expectations, with their personal preferences, or with their experiences in matching character to particular names?

Tom, Dick, or Harry? If the Tom you knew at school was an A* pupil, or Dick the harshest taskmaster you ever worked for, or Harry your first love who broke your heart, it will be difficult thereafter for you to dissociate those qualities from those names.

But it's not just our own personal memories that color our associations with a certain name; the actual sound the word itself gives off when it strikes the ear—brittle, tinny, soft, or sibilant, for example—creates its own resonance.

In numerology, each letter of the alphabet has a numerical equivalent, and, as such, every word may be converted into a number in just the same way that a date of birth is reduced to a single digit. This conversion produces what is known as an Expression Number, each locked within it a hidden vibrational influence. When decoded, the Expression Number of a name yields valuable insights into the power of its sound.

LETTER CONVERSION CHART

1	2	3	4	5	6	7	8	9
A	B	C	D	E	F	G	H	I
J	K	L	M	N	O	P	Q	R
S	T	U	V	W	X	Y	Z	

EXPRESSION NUMBERS

Converting your name into its Expression Number is a simple process using the Alphabet Conversion Chart. Again for this purpose, only the digits 1 to 9 are used, with each number encapsulating a Personality Profile.

Using the conversion chart, take all the names given to you at birth, each with its exact spelling, and convert each letter into its numerical equivalent. Add all the numbers, continuing to add double figures together until you have reduced the addition to a single digit. The Personality Profiles for each number are described below.

Example

	S A R A H	E L I Z A B E T H	J O N E S
	1+1+9+1+8	5+3+9+8+1+2+5+2+8	1+6+5+5+1
	= 2+0	= 4 + 3	= 1 + 8
	= 2	= 7	= 9
Total	2 + 7 + 9	= 1 + 8	= 9

Thus, the Expression Number for the name Sarah Elizabeth Jones is NINE. By continuing to use all three names, Sarah projects the image and persona encapsulated by the characteristics resonated by the number NINE.

But supposing she prefers to use her middle name, Elizabeth, or even to shorten that further to Lizzy? Would that change how she feels about herself or how she comes across to other people?

	L I Z Z Y	J O N E S
	3 + 9 + 8 + 8 + 7	1 + 6 + 5 + 5 + 1
	= 3 + 5	= 1 + 8
	= 8	= 9
Total	8 + 9	= 1 + 7 = 8

As Lizzy Jones, Sarah projects a totally different persona: that of a number EIGHT personality.

Suppose, having established your Expression Number, you don't care for the character sketch this describes? Suppose you don't like your name at all and have wanted all your life to change it? Suppose for professional reasons you need a standout brand that will blaze a trail?

Fortunately, unlike a date of birth, it *is* possible to change a name, and people do so for all sorts of reasons. Nicknames are established, surnames may be exchanged in marriage, writers adopt pseudonyms, performers take on stage names.

What, one wonders, might have become of William Bradley Pitt (Expression Number FOUR) if he hadn't chosen to drop his first name and go by a foreshortened version of his middle name instead? As Brad Pitt he embodies, in a stroke of genius, the Expression Number EIGHT, symbol of good fortune and material prosperity.

And would Reginald Kenneth Dwight (Expression Number TWO) have achieved the stratospheric superstardom and wealth if he hadn't assumed the alternative identity as Elton John, which carries the sparkling Expression Number FIVE?

Imponderable questions. But, in the same way, if you don't like your name or if you're unhappy with your lot in life, you might like to consider a name change too. By changing your name, you will begin to express a new personality that will create a different impression and thereby attract a whole new set of reactions and circumstances to yourself. But it needn't be such a dramatic step that would require a new form of identification. Something quite simple, such as a subtle change of spelling or a new diminutive form of your current name, might suffice to alter the overall Expression Number.

However, before embarking on any changes, first check out your current Expression Number, and if you're still dissatisfied, decide on the sort of image picture you want to project by reading through the Personality Profiles below and then work out a name for yourself that reduces to that number. Remember that you will never completely lose the underlying vibrational influence of your original name, but you can certainly overlay it as we have seen in the examples of both Brad Pitt and Elton John.

Finally, don't forget to consult the Table of Harmonies at the end of the chapter to confirm that either your current or your new Expression Number chimes harmoniously with your Destiny Number. If they do, there will be an easy interchange between your character and the way you function in life. If there is any discord between the two, it might be that you struggle to achieve your ambitions, or you feel you're constantly missing out, or that you're just not reaching your full potential. In that case, you could experiment with a change of name—it might alter the course of the rest of your life.

PERSONALITY PROFILES

EXPRESSION NUMBER 1

ONE is the number of independence and self-assertiveness. There is no mistaking these individuals, since they possess powerful and dominant personalities and make an impact on all those they meet.

Strong willed, self-sufficient, channeled, and direct, these people are born leaders. They are ambitious and are happier at the top than lower down the ranks, preferring to be at the front, where the action is, than bringing up the rear. Usually bright and intelligent, there is a strong element of originality and creativity in their makeup. Action is their keyword, either physical or intellectual, and those with an Expression Number ONE will be constantly on the go, filling their lives with a whirlwind of activity.

Their greatest faults lie in their egocentric preoccupation with themselves, which can lead to inconsiderate behavior toward others, to arrogance, and to a desire to dominate events, situations, and people.

EXPRESSION NUMBER 2

Whereas ONE is happier leading the cavalry charge, people with the Expression Number TWO prefer to be part of the support network, patiently waiting with the food and bandages on the touchline until their assistance is required. Passive and receptive, these people possess an abundance of sympathy and understanding, which makes them valuable partners and teammates. Indeed, they are never happy alone, since they prefer living and working with others, quietly dispensing the wisdom and experience they have acquired over years of sitting in the background and simply watching the human condition. In general shy and retiring, they are never comfortable pushing themselves forward but always prepared to cooperate and be carried along by the enthusiasm of others. Gentle, sensitive, and intuitive, these people always seek balance and harmony.

Their faults include excessive sensitivity, indecisiveness, and a tendency to be overdependent on others. Because they try so hard to avoid all forms of confrontation, they invariably end up sitting on the fence.

EXPRESSION NUMBER 3

Chatty, noisy, full of life, full of fun, THREE describes a happy, lively, gregarious individual. Those who possess this as their Expression Number are bright and friendly extroverts. Ever optimistic, enthusiastic, and appreciative of the joys and beauty that surround them, they spread color and cheer wherever they go. Self-expression is the key to understanding their personalities, and such people will naturally gravitate toward the arts, since they have highly imaginative and original ideas. These people are extremely talented and have no equals when it comes to creative and artistic flair; consequently Expression Number THREE will be found in the worlds of music and art and, particularly, in the media. The number THREE is an especially lucky number to possess.

Faults among this group lie mainly in a too-frivolous or too-superficial attitude toward life.

EXPRESSION NUMBER 4

Expression Number FOUR represents solidity and stability. This number represents honest, hardworking, responsible individuals, staunchly plowing through the day, following a set routine with dogged persistence. When it comes to manual dexterity and practical skills, these people are unbeatable. Meticulous over detail, practical, level headed, and down to earth, they may sometimes be accused of lacking imagination and originality, so they are at their best in the fields in which they can make full use of their immense common sense and logical mentality. Strongly authoritarian and firm believers in law and order, in the Establishment, and in the status quo, they make upright citizens. Workwise, Expression Number FOUR may be found in traditional institutions such as the police force, the legal system, armed services, banking, and the Civil Service. It is by dint of their persistence and determination that those owning this Expression Number are rewarded and eventually find success.

Faults with this group lie mainly in too strict an attitude to life, too stiff an upper lip so that they repress emotion, and a too-dull and plodding existence that lacks color and variety in their daily routines.

EXPRESSION NUMBER 5

Volatile, adaptable, and restless sums up those with an Expression Number FIVE. Above all else, these individuals are quick witted. They possess bright, mercurial mentalities that pick up new skills, new information, and new tricks at a mere glance. Because they are such fast learners, almost inspirational in their uptake, FIVES can become easily bored, requiring masses of variety and distraction to keep their interest from flagging. Their razor-sharp minds, too, become impatient, especially with punctilious detail, red tape, and crass stupidity. With their chameleonlike characters, owners of this Expression Number are changeable and therefore perhaps unreliable, often turning out to be the mavericks in the pack. And the search for constant distraction and stimulation applies equally to their need for variety in both activities and people in their lives. Among the mercurial occupations that so often attract this group, sales and marketing seem to be popular since this not only provides diversity but also creates the stimulus with which their butterfly minds can excel.

On the negative side, FIVES can be irresponsible and overindulgent. A Machiavellian urge to manipulate people and situations may also be a negative tendency.

EXPRESSION NUMBER 6

The true homemaker is symbolized by Expression Number SIX. People belonging to this group have a reputation for being emotionally stable, and, like FOURS, they tend to be solid and responsible individuals. SIXES are family oriented, lovers of hearth and home. Fairly creative, they admire gracious living and actively seek to create a pleasing and harmonious environment wherever they are, whether this is in the home or in the workplace. Kind and understanding, those whose names convert to the Expression Number SIX make excellent partners and caring parents. Since they have a strong sense of service, they will be found in all areas of the vocational and caring professions.

Negative characteristics involve jealousy, and, because these people often feel strongly that they know best, they do have a tendency to give others the benefit of their advice—whether they have been invited to do so or not.

EXPRESSION NUMBER 7

Those who belong to the Expression Number SEVEN group have inquiring minds. Fairly introspective types, they delight in quietly taking things apart in order to see how they work. This applies not only to inanimate objects but also to complex abstract principles, psychological concepts, and established belief systems. These people actively seek peace and quiet in which they can pursue their analytical trains of thought, and, as such, they prefer to work on their own rather than with others. Generally highly intelligent, they make excellent researchers, analysts, philosophers, and scientists and may be found in many intellectual professions and fields of endeavor. As individuals, however, SEVENS may be somewhat cool and aloof in their approach to others, and, because they don't readily open up or express their innermost feelings, they can all too easily be misunderstood.

Pitfalls include secretiveness and a tendency to repress emotion.

EXPRESSION NUMBER 8

People who fall into this group are highly achievement motivated, prepared to work day and night in order to amass their fortune and secure material prosperity. Excellent organizers and confident of their powers and abilities, they pursue their goal relentlessly and often ruthlessly too. The attainment of financial security seems to be uppermost in their minds, and they will brook little opposition or interference along the way. These are the executives, the bankers, the financiers, the managers, the wheeler-dealers, the men and women who control the purse strings of the economy. Wherever big business is taking place, there will be number EIGHT tightly holding the reins. Status, too, is important to them because this is the external manifestation of their wealth. So, grand financial schemes, commercial expertise, money, power, position, and as many of the material comforts that wealth will buy just about sums up the motivating principles underlying this Expression Number.

Negative aspects include a lack of sensitivity and an obsessive desire for power.

EXPRESSION NUMBER 9

The Expression Number NINE describes those with a strong altruistic and philanthropic streak to their nature. Unlike EIGHTS, whose efforts tend to be self-centered, NINES are true humanitarians who make it their life ambition to further the cause of humanity and to better the lot of mankind. Theirs is a broad, universal outlook, never insular or parochial; they seek as wide a range of experience as life has to offer. Busy, active people, they rush about cramming as much as they can into their day, though perhaps it is a characteristic of this group that they don't always achieve the sort of success their efforts deserve. But success can be attained, and often reward comes to them through their imaginative and creative endeavors. Expression Number NINE people are both spiritual and intellectual, with a strong tendency toward idealism. Charismatic individuals, they have the power to influence others and to fire them up with their own brand of enthusiasm and optimism. Consequently, they make excellent teachers, imparting their understanding and experiences with wisdom and compassion.

Faults attributable to this group include impatience—they can seriously champ at the bit and become extremely frustrated and even bitter if restricted or if they feel their efforts have not been suitably recognized or rewarded.

Table of Harmonies

EXPRESSION NUMBER	HARMONIOUS	AT VARIANCE
1	1,3,5,7	4,6
2	2,4,6,8	5,7
3	1,3,5,6,9	2,4
4	2,4,6,8	1,5,7
5	1,3,5	2,4,6
6	2,3,4,6,9	1,5,7
7	1,4,7	2,6,9
8	2,4,6,8	7
9	3,6,9	7

CHAPTER THREE

LOVE AND ATTRACTION

5 8 2 9 1 4 3 6 7

NUMBERS FALL INTO discrete

groups, and the way they relate to each other depends very much on the vibration each puts out as to whether it will harmonize, attract, or oppose another given number. There are three groups, each group containing three numbers that are in sync with one another and therefore in harmony within its set.

The first group belongs to the *Physical* category and contains the numbers **2**, **4**, and **8**.

The second is known as the *Emotional* group and contains the numbers **3**, **6,** and **9**.

The third set is called the *Mental* category and contains the numbers **1**, **5,** and **7**.

Numbers within the same group share an overall similarity in their nature and hence have a special affinity with each other. So, by calculating the numerical equivalent—or Expression Number—of two people, it will reveal whether or not the couple belongs to the same harmonic group—and perhaps go some way toward explaining how harmonious or otherwise their relationship together will be.

Some numerologists maintain that to correctly ascertain compatibility of the Expression Numbers involved, it is necessary to convert the entire list of names as given at birth.

Example

	ELEANOR	JESSICA	GRAY
	5+3+5+1+5+6+9	1+5+1+1+3+1	7+9+1+7
	= 34	= 12	= 24
	= 3 + 4 = 7	= 1 + 2 = 3	= 2 + 4 = 6
Total	7 + 3 + 6 =	16	1 + 6 = 7

Others, however, believe that when considering the question of attraction and compatibility, what counts are the names by which the individuals are more familiarly known. So, in this example, Eleanor Jessica Gray may indeed be on the birth certificate, but preferring to call herself Ellie Gray changes the vibrational influence she radiates.

Example

	ELLIE	GRAY
	5 + 3 + 3 + 9 + 5	7 + 9 + 1 + 7
	= 25	= 24
	= 2 + 5 = 7	= 2 + 4 = 6
Total	7 + 6 =	1 + 3 = 4

By modifying our names, we are in effect changing our brand, and this in turn has an effect on our personality. We assume different characteristics that perhaps are influenced by the tone or sound of that name or perhaps are reflected by other people's reactions or expectations upon introducing ourselves. So, Frederick, for example, is likely to behave or to be treated differently from Fred. Similarly, someone called Christine projects a different picture than would a person who presents herself as Chrissie.

So, do the numbers in your relationship spoon? Find out by comparing the Expression Numbers in your names and read on to discover what kind of a love match your numbers create. Here's a famous couple:

Example

	JULIET	CAPULET
	1 + 3 + 3 + 9 + 5 + 2	3 + 1 + 7 + 3 + 3 + 5 + 2
	= 2 + 3 = 5	= 2 + 4 = 6
Total	5 + 6 =	1 + 1 = 2

Example

	R O M E O	**M O N T A G U E**
	9 + 6 + 4 + 5 + 6	4 + 6 + 5 + 2 + 1 + 7 + 3 + 5
	= 3 + 0 = 3	= 3 + 3 = 6
Total	3 + 6 = 9	

Given their Expression Numbers of TWO and NINE, it is interesting to speculate: Had Romeo and Juliet's tragic fate not taken place, what sort of relationship might these two star-crossed lovers have had together! How do you and your partner respond to each other? Your Expression Numbers will throw light on the question. But remember in all your calculations that every relationship is unique, and the descriptions given here are very general. The magic and magnetism that draw two people together are complex and mysterious. Bear in mind, too, that each number is imbued with both positive and negative characteristics: none of us are perfect, nor indeed, all bad.

THE NUMBER ONE IN LOVE

People whose Expression Number is ONE need love and romance (with a capital R!) in their lives. They are adventurous people and make sensual and sexy partners. But they need more than just sex in their relationships; they need a meeting of minds too, so they will be looking for intellectual stimulation from their partners as well as true love. If they can't get the intellectual buzz, they may be tempted to look elsewhere.

More than anything, ONES hate to be pinned down. They feel stifled if they think their independence has been taken away from them, so unless they can maintain a certain sense of freedom within a relationship, they may simply spread their wings and seek wider horizons.

ONES are very proud people, and in any relationship they have to come out on top. They cannot bear to be criticized, and if they

are, they have a tendency to stonewall you. But it is their egotism and selfishness that are perhaps their most negative characteristics in a relationship and are most likely to upset the apple cart.

In Partnership

1 + 1 Though on the same wavelength, a couple of ONES in the same relationship are likely to constantly fight for supremacy.

1 + 2 ONES are physically attracted to TWOS, and it is true that TWOS need a strong partner in life, which ONES undoubtedly are. However, TWOS need pampering, plenty of love and understanding, and masses of togetherness, which after a while may tax the patience of the more adventurous and independent ONES.

1 + 3 This is an excellent combination. ONES are mentally and emotionally attracted to THREES, whose interesting and fun-loving attitude toward life provides a good complement to their needs and nature.

1 + 4 ONES may perhaps find FOURS just a little too stolid for their adventurous spirits. So perhaps as partnerships go, these two may find themselves all too often out of sync.

1 + 5 ONES are mentally and physically attracted to FIVES. This relationship has all the makings of a potentially exciting and stimulating partnership.

1 + 6 ONES are adventurous; SIXES are stay at home. ONES have a touch of irresponsibility; SIXES have a strong sense of duty. Sounds like these two are simply not on the same wavelength.

1 + 7 There's a strong mental attraction between these two. ONES find the coolness and aloofness that SEVEN presents an irresistible challenge that keeps them enthralled.

1 + 8 ONES are physically attracted to EIGHTS. These two can go a long way together, especially in business.

1 + 9 These two can form strong bonds of friendship together. Both are independent types, outgoing, and prone to intense emotions. So a good basis for a relationship here.

THE NUMBER TWO IN LOVE

People whose Expression Number reduces to TWO are sensitive and understanding. Because they are passive, especially sexually, they are best in a supportive role. They actively seek a loving relationship because they need a solid, reliable partner who they can respect and who will provide—physically, emotionally, and financially—a warm, stable, and secure nest. In return, they make responsive lovers and offer loyalty and devotion, a sympathetic ear, a charming, tactful, and adaptable nature, and a loving environment to return home to at the end of the day.

In general, members of this group are gentle and readily respond to kindness. Given tenderness, understanding, and appreciation, they visibly open up like flowers in the sun. A relationship based on teamwork and on cooperation is essential to them, since they are born to share and to please those they love. Above all else, TWOS love peace and harmony and will do their utmost to avoid quarrels or any form of discord in their domestic lives.

Because they hate hurting and upsetting others, TWOS may hang on in an unhappy relationship rather than make a clean break of it. Indeed, many among this group seem to experience more than their fair share of relationship problems, especially through the first half of their lives. Perhaps this is because some can become easy prey, easily taken advantage of, or perhaps it may be due to the fact that they have such idealistic expectations about their partners that they can all too easily feel let down.

In Partnership

2 + 1 TWOS are physically attracted to ONES, and they would provide the warm nest for ONES to return to. They certainly benefit from the strength of character that ONES would bring to the relationship, but it is debatable whether at the end of the day they would get all the personal support they need out of the partnership.

2 + 2 Because TWOS tend to be passive, responsive, and indecisive, some may consider this relationship somewhat unadventurous. They are, nevertheless, on the same wavelength.

2 + 3 TWOS seem to be physically and emotionally attracted to THREES since they find them lively and fun to be with. Perhaps, though, not so good as a long-term proposition because TWOS would feel insecure and undermined by the gregarious and flirtatious attitude of this partner.

2 + 4 These two are mentally and physically attracted to one another. This augurs an excellent combination with good long-term prospects.

2 + 5 Given their compliant nature, TWOS could all too easily fall under the spell of the stronger, more dazzling FIVE. But in this combination FIVES could prove careless, taking advantage of the devotion TWO gives.

2 + 6 A super combination with both needing the same things in life. Moreover, each is physically, mentally, and emotionally attracted to the other.

2 + 7 Although TWOS may be physically attracted to SEVENS, this combination may lack the sort of nurturing warmth that TWOS require.

2 + 8 Could work well, since TWOS will give EIGHTS the loyalty, devotion, and dedication of an emotionally supportive partner. In return, EIGHTS would provide the material security that is fundamental to this relationship.

2 + 9 On a physical level these two could be attracted to each other. But there may be too many differences of opinion to guarantee long-term success: TWOS tend to be inward looking, while NINES look outward, so TWOS may prove too parochial for NINES, who have the universe at their feet.

THE NUMBER THREE IN LOVE

THREES tend to gravitate to center stage, since they are born extroverts and are seekers after the limelight. As partners they are lively and interesting, witty and fun loving, infecting all those around them with their own special brand of cheerfulness and enthusiasm. Never dull, they are blessed with a marvelous sense of humor, and if you're feeling low, just leave it to your THREE partner to pick you up and make you laugh again.

Friendship is especially important to them, since they are naturally gregarious types—if partnered with a number THREE, your home will probably be filled with a constant stream of people coming and going. Friendship is also essential in their personal relationships, and this has to be at the very core of any loving or sexual partnership they form. For them, marriage has to be a true partnership in every sense of the word.

When it comes to romantic interactivity, THREES seem to possess a certain inborn flirtatiousness, especially when young, and as a result may find it difficult to commit themselves and settle down. They have an idealistic view of marriage, and once they find a partner who is happy-go-lucky, prepared to flatter them, lavish them with love, affection, and attention, and, moreover, tolerate their petty foibles, THREES will commit themselves happily and return every bit of love they are blessed to receive.

In Partnership

3 + 1 Good rapport between these two. Fairly well on the same wavelength, each is mentally and emotionally attracted to the other. A potentially zingy relationship.

3 + 2 THREES could benefit from TWO's lavish attention but in time would feel frustrated and even held back by TWO's passivity and need for security and stability. TWOS may well suffer from THREE's cavalier attitude in any close personal relationship.

3 + 3 A relationship full of sparkle and fun, but perhaps not enough seriousness here to tackle the nitty-gritty of everyday life.

3 + 4 Seemingly difficult, although there would be some advantages to both parties if the relationship were handled intelligently. Solid and dependable, FOURS would gain from THREE's lightheartedness in life, while THREES would benefit from FOUR's stability. But with the wrong pair, it would be chalk and cheese.

3 + 5 Brilliant all-around partnership. Mentally challenging, physically exciting, emotionally and sexually stimulating. Full of activity, masses of variety, and plenty of buzz.

3 + 6 A good combination. Both in harmony with each other, and both mentally and physically attracted to one another. SIX happily takes care of the domestic arrangements while THREE contributes the sparkle to the relationship.

3 + 7 Perhaps not ideal as a long-term union. Though there could be a meeting of minds, there would be precious little else coming together between these two.

3 + 8 This relationship has great potential, especially if in business together and if each respects and allows the other's talents to flourish. When the combination works, it can be a materially and financially successful team.

3 + 9 Good harmony should exist between these two, THREES and NINES being physically and mentally attracted to one another. On a deeply personal level, though, would NINES find THREES spiritually insensitive? And could THREES put up with NINE's constant need for humanitarian fulfillment?

THE NUMBER FOUR IN LOVE

FOURS are eminently dependable and reliable. They are hardworking and eager to provide stability and security for those they love. Although not naturally spontaneous at social mixing—they find it difficult to make friends—they are, nevertheless, very affectionate toward those they love. Since FOURS are not especially gregarious, domestic life is all the more important to them, dearly loving their partners, children, and homes.

In long-term relationships, FOURS make conscientious, loyal, and faithful partners. Fair minded, honest, and sincere, they like to build their relationships upon the solid foundations of good, old-fashioned values. These people are born with broad shoulders, tailor-made upon which they willingly place the burdens of responsibility in life. The problem is that they do tend to work too hard, almost verging on the workaholic. They have to learn to make more space for their leisure pursuits and to enjoy some good-quality time with their families.

An intellectual mate with a lively mind makes an ideal partner. However, although FOURS admire strength of character in a partner, they cannot tolerate being dominated or overshadowed, which consequently can lead to a certain amount of discord. Perhaps, though, the most-important qualities that a partner to a FOUR should possess are cheerfulness and a ready wit. Someone, in effect, who is prepared to show their number FOUR lover the lighter side of life and remind them occasionally not to take life (in general) and themselves (in particular) quite so seriously.

In Partnership

4 + 1 Apart from needing physical comforts in life and sharing good business sense, there is little else in common here.

4 + 2 Excellent relationship with a strong mental understanding and physical attraction. FOURS provide the material security, while TWOS bring their sensitivity and responsiveness to the partnership.

4 + 3 Rather disparate types, although if they found a true meeting ground, each would benefit enormously from the other. FOURS are conservative and industrious, while THREES are fun loving and flirtatious with life, so FOURS could supply the material security and THREES the interest and tonic to bring the relationship alive.

4 + 4 A strong solid relationship, happy in their own sphere. Lots of hard work, lots of seriousness, and consequently lots of material and financial success. Plodding, stolid union but perhaps with few heady heights.

4 + 5 Success for this combination may be hard to sustain. FOURS need a solid, stable relationship, but FIVES simply can't be pinned down.

4 + 6 A splendid match. SIXES are the domestic homemakers and excellent parents whom FOURS need as a backup in their lives.

4 + 7 Though potentially promising as a creative meeting of minds, SEVENS are too cool, too aloof, and too untenable for solid, down-to-earth FOURS, making this a difficult pairing.

4 + 8 Brilliant relationship right across the board, with masses of mental and physical attraction. Both high achievers, so there is every prospect for a successful and prosperous life together.

4 + 9 Important difference in points of view here. FOURS are inward looking and could find NINE's global view uncomfortable. NINES need a broad-minded partner, and FOURS might prove a little too narrow for them.

THE NUMBER FIVE IN LOVE

Clever, sharp, quick witted, streetwise, FIVES are great wanderers, adventurers, and travelers. More than anything else in life, they loathe the idea of being stuck in a rut, treading the same groove from 9 to 5, day in and day out. New horizons, change, variety, always having to be one step ahead is the thrill, the charge that FIVES need to keep them stimulated, to keep that adrenalin flowing in their veins.

And they need the same sort of adventure and excitement when it comes to matters of the heart. More than any of the other Expression Numbers, FIVES are sensual creatures, prone to overindulgence of physical pleasures and ruled by a strong sex drive.

Although in their youth, their curiosity and roving nature lead to their many love affairs, when FIVES do finally settle down, it will be with someone who shares their sense of romance, who will love their children, and who are happy to provide a warm home for their return. Moreover, it will be to someone who will offer a challenge, provide a mental stimulus, and perhaps be prepared to accept an easy, open type of relationship. Their partners will learn to accommodate that restless impulse, that sense of freedom and need for independence. They will recognize that what FIVES ultimately seek is emotional fulfillment.

In Partnership

5 + 1 What an exciting, stimulating, and fizzy relationship! Each is mentally, physically, and sexually attracted to the other. The only snag is, does either of these have time to be truly understanding and sympathetic of the other, or, when the chips are down, is each too egocentric or self-absorbed to really care?

5 + 2 Difficulties would soon show up with these two. TWOS tend to be clinging and demanding and need more protection and security than FIVES are prepared to give. Additionally, FIVES could all too easily take advantage of TWO's yielding and more passive nature.

5 + 3 Great attraction between these two, and perhaps one of the best combinations for FIVES, filled with sexual frisson and excitement. In fact, life is just one great big bowl of cherries for this couple.

5 + 4 Different needs, different ideas, different purpose in life. FOURS like routine, but FIVES are too casual and need constant change and variety. Hence somewhat of a mismatch here.

5 + 5 On the same wavelength, with plenty of excitement and a life filled with passionate highs and lows. However, each is too busy doing their own thing, which mitigates for a mutually receptive togetherness.

5 + 6 If SIXES were prepared to be tolerant, accepting of FIVE's vagaries, and prepared to make a nice warm nest ready for FIVE's return, the relationship could work well. In reality, though, FIVE finds SIX stifling, while SIX considers FIVE to be irresponsible.

5 + 7 Inasmuch as SEVENS like their own company and FIVES are always out and about, it would seem that these two would make few unreasonable demands on the other. When they do come together, however, they have a great deal to say to each other. Though not the makings of an emotionally close relationship, these two can enjoy a vibrantly stimulating mental rapport.

5 + 8 Good for business, making for a constructive and successful partnership. For a closer union, though, FIVES would have to show a good deal more responsibility in order to keep EIGHT's attention, and EIGHTS would have to spend less time at work and more together time with FIVES in order to keep the interest alive.

5 + 9 Potentially good all-around. A stimulating, interesting, lively partnership. Plenty of mental and physical attraction with enjoyably zingy sex.

THE NUMBER SIX IN LOVE

Domestic and home loving, SIXES prefer not to live alone. They are very affectionate, loving types for whom a happy family and close relationship are essential to their well-being. Nothing makes a SIX happier than being needed, because people with this Expression Number are born to help others, to be of service not only to their immediate family but also to the community at large.

As partners, SIXES are thoroughly dependable, responsible, sympathetic, and generous to a fault. They have a tendency to be somewhat idealistic about love, romance, and long-term relationships. Perhaps all too ready to don those rose-colored specs and dream about roses around the cottage door. Certainly, they do have a habit of placing their loved ones on pedestals and blinding themselves to their faults.

At home they are excellent at keeping house, efficient with the housekeeping, and good at all domestic activities. They are the sort who are able to somehow magically transform a house into a home—they make splendid cooks, are creatively gifted when it comes to interior decorating, and are blessed with green thumbs so that their gardens bloom and their houseplants prosper. Many are even able to sing beautifully or play a musical instrument (or both) to soothe the family after a stressful working day.

It is said that of all the Expression Numbers, SIXES generally make the best parents. With wisdom and good sense, they bring up their children in a tolerant, caring, and nurturing environment, take their education in hand, and are generally concerned about their welfare. But perhaps the criticism that might be leveled at these models of partner and parenthood is that they can all too often become possessive and overprotective, and that many of them fall into the self-righteous trap of thinking that they always know what is best for others.

In Partnership

6 + 1 Quite a few difficulties are likely to arise between these two Expression Numbers in a close relationship. SIXES need more domestic security and commitment than ONES may be prepared to offer, while independent ONES could find their SIX partner overwhelmingly possessive.

6 + 2 A great combination. A compatible union arguing well for long-term success together. Each sympathetic and responsive to the other, both pulling together with the same aims and objectives in life.

6 + 3 A winning team. Together, these two go far. Mental, physical, and emotional compatibility here. SIXES are happy to provide backup security for THREES, while THREES bring home the pizzazz that adds the color and interest to the relationship.

6 + 4 Another winner! Together these augur a solid, hardworking, caring, and productive coupling. They share conventional views and responsible attitudes toward life.

6 + 5 Chalk and cheese, these two. SIXES need commitment, but restless FIVES can't bear to be pinned down. Additionally, SIXES may be too conservative for the devil-may-care attitude of FIVES.

6 + 6 Similar types with similar aims in life. But what happens when either one thinks they *know* what's best for the other?

6 + 7 Little to unite these two. SIXES may prove too warm and clingy for cool, aloof SEVENS. SEVENS are far too impersonal for cuddly SIX.

6 + 8 A very good combination. SIXES would provide all the domestic warmth and understanding that EIGHTS need, while EIGHTS provide all the material security in which SIXES can fulfill their creative talents.

6 + 9 A sympathetic relationship, each partner in tune and in harmony with the other. Masses of mental mind-touch, good for business and for creative and emotional fulfillment.

THE NUMBER SEVEN IN LOVE

Those in a long-term relationship with someone whose name number is a SEVEN will know how difficult it is to penetrate the inner sanctum of this partner's thoughts. Indeed, SEVENS are complex personalities, reserved, sensitive, and aloof. "Still waters . . . " describes them very well, and because they have a tendency to guard their thoughts, contain their emotions, and generally keep themselves to themselves, they are often misunderstood. Getting SEVENS to talk about their innermost feelings is like pushing a megaton boulder up a 1:5 gradient.

Since they appear so cool and aloof on first meeting them, SEVENS are difficult to approach and even more so to warm to. In greeting, they would shun kissing and hugging—billing and cooing is definitely not their style.

And talking of which, style is something SEVENS have in abundance. These are the most cultured and refined individuals, with elegance and good taste reflected in their homes and environments. Everything here will be artistic and decorative, and even if they can't afford much, there will nevertheless be a sense of high quality, since they possess an exquisite eye for detail. There is rarely confusion or clutter in the number SEVEN's household, because they imbue their homes with a sense of calmness, order, and harmony.

Just as they are discriminating about their homes, so they are equally selective when it comes to affairs of the heart, and in general SEVENS marry well. And because they choose their partners so carefully, once committed, they tend to remain faithful. Their partners, however, must learn to live with SEVEN's need for solitude and allow them some time to themselves in the day, time to get away from the noise and the hurly-burly of modern life, to quietly gather their thoughts together and to recharge their spiritual, mental, and emotional batteries.

In Partnership

7 + 1 There is good mental harmony between these two, since they can enjoy an intellectual charge from each other. On a platonic level, then, there is a great deal of compatibility of temperament, but in a romantic context, SEVENS could well find ONES dominant and overbearing, turned off by their emotional ardor.

7 + 2 Potentially, there could be some irritation here. SEVENS are cool and seemingly unresponsive toward TWOS, who need closeness and support.

7 + 3 A relationship with a lot of merit, although at first perhaps not quite so apparent. Plenty of creative spin-off coupled with a good deal of mental and physical attraction. Only snag might arise from THREE's love of social company in comparison to SEVEN's need for solitude.

7 + 4 A good match. Neither is superficial or gregarious. FOURS would benefit from SEVEN's love of research, while SEVENS could find that FOURS are able to translate their ideas into practical reality for them.

7 + 5 Though potentially a good amount of mind touch, apart from a possible business partnership there could be a lack of common ground upon which SEVENS and FIVES could build a solid close relationship. FIVES are considered far too superficial by deeper-thinking SEVENS.

7 + 6 SIXES need a warm, domestic, and secure environment in which to make their homes and nurture their offspring. Moreover, SIXES need a strong network of friends around to give them support. These are the very needs that would irritate SEVENS, who are not at all social types or in the least domestically inclined. This, then, is not an auspicious recipe for long-term happiness.

7 + 7 Two people in harmony with each other, sharing similar tastes and similar talents. But because both are introspective, there is the possibility that neither would have time to give the other attention or make the effort to discuss their innermost feelings with one another.

7 + 8 A difficult combination here, EIGHT being materialistic and worldly wise while SEVEN is soul seeking and withdrawn.

7 + 9 There's a chance that this could be a workable combination. Both are independent types and would respect the other's need for spiritual fulfillment. But on a more personal basis, they would have to reach a certain level of understanding if the relationship were to be viable. The reason being that SEVENS could seem a little too detached, while NINES might be considered uncaring by their partner. However, a strong physical attraction might just be enough to bond them together.

THE NUMBER EIGHT IN LOVE

EIGHTS are not exactly sentimental. Seldom carried away by romantic ideals, they are supreme realists. When it comes to affairs of the heart, they know full well that love in poverty is a recipe for disaster.

People whose names have a numerical value of EIGHT are materialists through and through. They thrive on success and on the sort of secure and comfortable life that money will provide. They are very much creatures of comfort and are prepared to work hard to get what they want out of life. Some EIGHTS with a more worldly practicality may actively look to marry into money.

Material success and all the trimmings that go with it—status symbols, influential friends, prestigious acquaintances—are all important to this Expression Number, who seems to naturally gravitate toward people of the same ilk. Workwise, they are likely to be in big business or run their own company, and prospective partners are often met among people in the same line of work. In fact, many EIGHTS work best together, perhaps in a joint business venture or as partners in a family concern.

Essentially, EIGHTS need to marry someone they respect, someone strong whom they can admire and who will provide the solid foundation and material security they require. Often, EIGHTS form relationships where there is a wide disparity in age. Generally, it appears they find true happiness either when they marry someone much older than themselves, or when they settle down with their chosen partner later on in life, toward middle age.

Once married or committed to a partner, those in this category deeply love their spouses, children, and homes. They especially love animals, who are very much considered additional members of the family, so expect to find several pets here to complete this warm nest.

In Partnership

8 + 1 Good potential for a materially successful relationship. Both parties are ambitious go-getters so are likely to achieve their aims in life. In a romantic relationship, though, each is as bossy as the other, so look out for occasional fireworks!

8 + 2 A good mutually receptive relationship. EIGHTS provide the material security, and TWOS bring the spiritual backup and support.

8 + 3 Good prospects for this combination, especially if they are in business together. These two seem to be physically attracted, and on all levels of interaction EIGHTS provide the executive abilities while THREES add the glamour, status, and pizzazz that lifts and lends interest to the relationship. Good for as long as it lasts.

8 + 4 A well-matched pair. These two are on the same wavelength, both prepared to work hard shoulder to shoulder to achieve their aims and ambitions in life. The only slight snag is that this relationship, concentrating as it does on all work and no play, is in danger of becoming dull and stolid. A touch of color and excitement now and again helps invigorate and refresh this pairing.

8 + 5 Technically an interesting match, especially if they are in business together, where EIGHTS are the executives and FIVES front the public image. In the domestic situation, however, EIGHTS might be too engrossed in their work to give their partners the attention and personal satisfaction they need. In their turn, FIVES could be seen as too restless and flighty by their more responsible partners.

8 + 6 An excellent liaison. Plenty of mind touch, physical attraction, with both wanting the same things in life. Both prepared to support the other in their achievement of their aims on all levels of their relationship.

8 + 7 Aims and ambitions wide apart between these two, so potentially a mismatch here.

8 + 8 This has all the elements of a prosperous celebrity-type relationship. Together, these two have the Midas touch.

8 + 9 Potentially a good deal of physical attraction here, with each benefiting the other by working together. On a deeper personal level, EIGHTS may not be broad minded and tolerant enough for NINE's humanitarian pursuits, while NINES could well find their partner's materialistic attitudes somewhat philosophically narrow.

THE NUMBER NINE IN LOVE

To belong to the Expression Number NINE means being part of the brotherhood of humanity. NINES are spiritual creatures, generous in their emotional idealism and with broad philosophical views on life that transcend nations and boundaries. Open minded and tolerant, they are caring and compassionate people, big hearted and liberal to a fault.

As partners, NINES are sympathetic and understanding, but they are independent types and will suffer if their freedom is denied them. And because they have such a wide perspective, they need a partner who is equally broad minded and prepared to take a global view of things. Anyone insular and narrow in outlook simply will not complement a NINE personality.

Immensely loving and giving (in fact, they may be described as "life's givers"), they gladly give themselves and all they possess to the ones they love. When it comes to matters of the heart, NINES are highly idealistic and tend to be in love with love. For them, falling in love is total, and when they do, they fall completely head over heels. They crave love and affection to such an extent that they will either meet and marry the partner of their dreams very early on in life or suffer many unhappy experiences when young, simply because they mistakenly give their hearts too readily to the wrong people.

Theirs is an idealistic view of life, and if their partners or their homes do not match up to these ideals, then that love, despite its original intensity, will soon dissipate. The sort of home life that might be described as "kitchen sink" is definitely not for NINES. It isn't that they require a palace or even great wealth for their happiness; it is simply that people, situations, and places must come up to the NINE's standards of excellence and must match their sense of aesthetics, goodness, and loveliness.

As parents, NINES will impart these high values to their children. Sternly disapproving of any low or underhanded behavior, they teach their youngsters morality and the importance of good manners and good breeding. NINES are especially fond of children, treating them as part of the universal family, the seeds of the future that form the links and the network of humankind.

Moreover, they are excellent homemakers, turning their hands to almost anything. With their artistic and creative abilities, they can transform a shabby environment into a comfortable, attractive, and pleasing place in which to live. And because they take a global view of life, their homes will have a cosmopolitan feel, with a mixture of styles and designs, filled with treasures lovingly brought back from their travels around the world.

In Partnership

9 + 1 Lively and stimulating relationship. Sexy and exciting. ONES have breath of vision and are cosmopolitan enough to respect NINE's far-reaching mentality.

9 + 2 Fairly good on a mental level, particularly when it comes to the exchange of creative ideas. On a more intimate level, NINES may find TWO's vision of life somewhat narrow and restricting.

9 + 3 A great match. Interesting, fun loving, buzzing, sparkling, and sexy too. But in their heart of hearts there will be times when NINE finds THREE's attitude just a little too superficial.

9 + 4 As much positive as negative with this couple, depending on the individuals concerned. NINES bring creative inspiration while FOURS add practical know-how. Together they could make a formidable team, putting ideas into reality, but there are times when stolid FOURS may lack the understanding of NINE's wider panoramic view of life.

9 + 5 A magnetic attraction between these two. A lively and exciting relationship with plenty of variety and interests to share. Perhaps FIVES are not quite as deep as NINES would like at times, but there are plenty of other compensations to keep the partnership alive.

9 + 6 Two Expression Numbers that are harmoniously suited right across the board. A very compatible union.

9 + 7 Perhaps not a great deal in common here to sustain matters in the long term.

9 + 8 Plenty going for these two if they handle it well. Good for business and for the exchange of ideas. Physical attraction between them helps. On an intimate level, EIGHTS tend to be unsentimental, while NINES are romantic. If each can make allowances for these differences of character, then there's a strong chance of success, especially if the interests are on an international scale.

9 + 9 These two are certainly on the same wavelength, sharing the same aims and objectives in life. Highly tipped for a successful relationship, and if they work together for humanitarian organizations, so much the better.

CHAPTER FOUR

WORK AND MONEY

CIRCUMSTANCES, opportunity, and luck play an integral part in the choice of work a person takes up. We don't all have the good fortune to pursue a career that satisfies or fulfills all our desires and skills. Finances, the need to pay our bills, and availability of jobs so often determine how we make our living.

With all things equal, however, most of us somehow or other do seem to gravitate to those occupations that have some bearing on our own interests and abilities. A person who enjoys the outdoors, for example, would not be happy, or perform at their best, cooped up in an office environment all day long. Nor would someone who can't stand heights choose to work as a scaffolder, steeplejack, or mountaineer.

In the workplace, some people are born leaders with broad shoulders able to take responsibility. Others, preferring to stand on the sidelines, are born followers, ever ready to lend support. Some are independent decision makers, needing to be their own boss. Others fare better in a corporate environment working as part of a team. And when it comes to money, there are those who are carefree with their cash, and others who are diligent savers. Some people are born with the Midas touch, effortlessly attracting wealth like a magnet, while it is the fate of others to roll up their sleeves and graft for their living.

Bearing in mind that there are always exceptions to the rule, numerology can give specific clues as to our abilities, whether technical, creative, practical, imaginative, or whatever. Whether you need help to choose the most appropriate occupation or find the best career route to develop your talents and make the most of your opportunities, your Destiny and Expression Numbers can light the way. These personal numbers can also hint at your financial prowess. But remember, as with Louise Ciccone, who found fame and wealth by changing her name to Madonna, or Maurice Micklewhite, who became the megastar Michael Caine, you too could spin the wheel of fortune your way by changing your Expression Number to one you feel would more suitably match your desired path in life.

DESTINY OR EXPRESSION NUMBER ONE AT WORK

People belonging to this group are born leaders, with all the qualities that are needed to take them to the top of whatever occupation they choose to follow in life. Just as ONE is the first of all numbers, so members of this tribe are usually found first in the queue and ahead of the game.

As a number, ONE in the workplace confers to its subjects power and independence. Ambition is a key driver, and, as a person with an abundance of confidence and self-assurance, success is never in doubt. It is their keen instinct that enables them to spot the opportunities that others miss, and, once spotted, they know how to make the very best of that gap in the market. Once they have that aim in mind, they will go "hell for leather" until they achieve their goal.

Whether as a birth or name number, ONES are tremendous planners: they make, create, and innovate. So they are likely to be found in research and development, in planning departments, and in business and commerce. And since they have the talent to inspire others and instill confidence, they make excellent teachers, counselors, advisors, and generals.

Wherever they work, ONES are at their best when they are in charge, in a commanding or supervisory capacity. Since they prefer to give, rather than take, orders or advice, they are best suited to either heading up a department or running their own business. And although they can suffer with tunnel vision at times and may be intolerant of anything that smacks of indolence, they do generally enjoy good relations with their staff.

Financially, money is not top of the list for people in this group, since their focus is more on love and personal success. Generally, their wealth is accrued through their inventive work and original start-ups and ideas.

DESTINY OR EXPRESSION NUMBER TWO AT WORK

People belonging to this group make excellent negotiators. Diplomatic, tactful, and cooperative, they are the essential go-betweens: skilled mediators in discussions or wherever arguments require a resolution.

Those whose birth or name number reduces to TWO do not crave the limelight as others might. They do not strive for the top job nor do they seek outright control. Instead, they find a satisfying niche in a supporting role, as the second in command, deputy leader, or vice president of a company.

Among their colleagues, TWOS tend to be helpful and kind and have an inborn knack of making others feel at ease. Where decision-making is concerned, TWOS unfailingly see both sides of the coin and, as such, do well in the justice or legal profession, as advisors, counselors, or union reps.

Because for them, service is a driver, so many will gravitate toward the health profession, social work, or charities. Their genuine understanding of what makes other people tick draws them to medicine and especially into the fields of psychology and psychiatry. Service in the form of catering also appeals, many becoming fine cooks and chefs. On a wider context, this leads to caring for the land, farming and agriculture, or tending to flora and fauna.

An eye for detail is a salient characteristic among those belonging to this group. That, together with a sensitivity to color and sound, endows TWOS with creative flair, which many develop either professionally or for personal pleasure through art or music. Playing an instrument or creating artwork is again seen as service, bringing enjoyment to others and adding a quintessential value to their own lives.

Financially, TWOS are honest and upright and therefore make trusted financial advisors. Indeed, many are found in banking. Personally, security is uppermost for them, so a nest egg tucked away for that rainy day gives them peace of mind.

DESTINY OR EXPRESSION NUMBER THREE AT WORK

People belonging to this group have a way with words. That's why they are drawn to the expressive arts: diarists, journalists, writers. As communicators par excellence, they populate the world of the media and may be found broadcasting on the radio or TV or having a myriad of avid followers reading their blogs. Social media is the playground of those whose birth or name number equates to THREE.

Multitalented, creative, and versatile, THREES can turn their hand to any occupation that involves talking and dealing with the general public. That's why they are so sought after in sales. They thrive in those jobs that involve travel, where situations constantly change, and where they have to think on their feet. And if they can work outdoors, so much the better.

Since the mission in life of the number THREE is to increase knowledge, members of this group make excellent teachers and lecturers. As well as imparting their own knowledge and experience to others, they are themselves eternal students forever reading and wanting to learn about new things.

Busy, busy, busy is the mantra of THREES, who have a tendency to dabble widely but perhaps not to dig too deeply into any one subject. Where this group succeeds and gives great value is in those occupations such as grand designs that favor an eye for the wide perspective or a sweep with a broad brush rather than those that require focus. Being regimented or working to routine does not bring out the best in those who belong to this group.

Financially, these people tend to be lucky. Knowing this makes them a little profligate with money. They can, however, generate wealth online, make a good living as brand or corporate influencers, and excel in after-dinner speaking. Making money for number THREE natives is one thing. Keeping it is another!

DESTINY OR EXPRESSION NUMBER FOUR AT WORK

People belonging to this group are makers, menders, conservators, and repairers. They are described as the salt of the earth: solid, reliable, honest, and dependable. It is their practical ability, the skill they have in any occupation that demands manual dexterity, that is not only their forte but also their path to success.

These are the pragmatic realists, the people who keep their—and our—feet on the ground: the builders, farmers, and engineers who furnish how we live, eat, shelter, and survive.

Persistence is their watchword. More than all the others, members of this group are the unsung heroes who stick at it day in and day out until they achieve what they set out to do. No matter how delicate, involved, dirty, or dire the situation is, they roll up their sleeves and get stuck in.

Being passionate about nature and the environment, managing from everyday homes to grand palatial estates, they excel in all domestic matters: efficiency, conservation, and preservation being key to their raison d'être. Always keen to pass on their skills, FOURS make excellent tutors in technical, building, or agricultural colleges. Students, however, are expected to follow the rules and work by the book.

People in this category like to be their own boss, to do things their own way—invariably they are right to do so. Because they are stubborn, their aim is to succeed sometimes against the odds, and they won't give up until they do.

Financially, people belonging to this group generally work hard for their living. Because money is carefully and slowly accrued and saved, they tend not to take risks with their cash. For them, building security is so important that they all too often forgo the pleasures in life that others enjoy. For members of this group, money is hard won and therefore precious.

DESTINY OR EXPRESSION
NUMBER FIVE AT WORK

People belonging to this group are the world's entertainers. Whether it involves spectators in an arena, listeners in an auditorium, or students in a classroom, FIVES are at their best when in front of an audience.

As speakers, FIVES have the gift of the gab and thrive when in the company of others. They can give inspirational pep talks, rally the troops with their persuasive words, and gather followers wherever they go. Since for them variety is key, FIVES relish any job that keeps them on the move, such as sales, lecture tours, or live appearances that involve traveling from venue to venue.

Born performers, the destiny of those who belong to the FIVE group is to cheer the rest of us up. In that respect, many FIVES are drawn to show biz: theater, television, and films. Since they are blessed with originality, making a name—and a fortune—for themselves on social media is not unusual.

Gifted artists energetic, extroverted, and colorful, their creative ideas can take them to the top of their chosen professions, whether in the arts, the music industry, or sports. And because FIVES are at ease when communicating, telling stories and imparting wisdom, the literary world is another draw, many excelling in journalism and publishing.

If not performing themselves, FIVES make formidable agents liaising between clients and taking special delight on the social circuit by mixing business with pleasure. They like nothing better than to be seen at glittering galas, award ceremonies, and celebrity parties. Burnout can be a problem among this group when enthusiasm gets the better of them. So FIVES must learn to pace themselves to avoid exhaustion.

Financially, money and romance are interwoven in these people's wealth-making; whether they win the lottery, write a blockbusting love story, or marry a multimillionaire, luck plays a big part in FIVE's happy fortunes.

DESTINY OR EXPRESSION NUMBER SIX AT WORK

People belonging to this group go about their duties in quiet self-effacing ways. Known for their creativity mixed with compassion, SIXES strive to create beauty, peace, and harmony in whatever occupation they find themselves.

Education, medicine, and welfare in general attract the number SIX, since essentially these are the carers in the community. As teachers, they care for the young and as medical practitioners they care for the sick. They are found in nursery schools, hospitals, clinics, and residential establishments for the elderly. Many train as dentists, podiatrists, pharmacists, and other allied clinical professions, including alternative therapies and working in health stores.

With well-being as a main driver, SIXES are drawn to those occupations that involve nurturing in its broadest sense. The beauty business, such as hairdressing, cosmetics, and perfumery, attracts many, as does fashion designing and sales—all those essential occupations that make us look and feel better.

At heart, SIXES are homemakers who find great satisfaction in those careers that involve houses and real estate, such as architecture, hotel management, and interior decorating. As part of creating a pleasing environment in which to live, many choose to work in horticulture, floristry, and garden design. Since catering also forms part of the love of domestic life, it is no surprise to find SIXES in the kitchen as cooks, chefs, and restauranteurs.

Once they take on a job, SIXES stick to it through thick and thin until they have accomplished what they set out to do. They find change disturbing, so consequently they tend not to move from job to job. Familiarity is comfortable for them, which makes SIX a reliable member of the workforce.

Financially, SIXES tend not to chase after fame and wealth. For them, the center of their universe is their home and family. As long as they earn enough—with a little spare for that proverbial rainy day—to provide for their loved ones and to keep their nests safe and secure, they are happy.

DESTINY OR EXPRESSION NUMBER SEVEN AT WORK

People belonging to this group like to work under their own steam, preferably alone or, if necessary, at least within a very small group. SEVENS are thinkers, diagnosticians, philosophers, scientists, and, in many cases, psychics—which puts them ahead of the game.

SEVENS like to dig and delve. Whatever is hidden or mysterious, whatever needs to be uncovered, or whatever has a question mark against it is irresistible to the probing minds of these people. It is the desire to seek the truth that turns this group into brilliant investigators.

They thrive when working in a laboratory on forensic research, when seeking that missing link, or when following clues to get to the answer. Intellectually, SEVENS glory in the conceptual realm, losing themselves in abstract metaphysical thought streams. They are especially in their element when unraveling long-held secrets or unlocking the mysteries of life. Their mission is to prove the unprovable. Ultimately, they yearn to discover the elixir of life. BUT, they must be left to their own devices without having to obey rules and regulations. That is why SEVENS make such good private investigators, inventors, or explorers who find their own way through untrodden territory.

Theoretical rather than practical, these are not team players. As a result, colleagues and workmates may find SEVENS distant, unapproachable, difficult to get along with. In every way, they are unconventional. Even their interests in transcendental matters and the occult, in which many SEVENS dabble successfully, are considered otherworldly and thus adding to their mystique.

Financially, members of this group are not the most practical when it comes to budgeting their money. If they have it, they spend it, and if they don't have it, they go without. Sporadically, SEVENS can be unexpectedly lucky: either they may inherit, receive a sizable lump-sum payment out of the blue, or even win the lottery. When this happens, they would be wise to find a trusty advisor to help them handle the windfall.

DESTINY OR EXPRESSION
NUMBER EIGHT AT WORK

People belonging to this group are ambitious. Whatever their starting position, they aim for the top, and sooner or later—usually sooner— they get there. It's because they are born with executive abilities and big ideas spurring them on from the get-go that gives EIGHTS that innate self-confidence to succeed.

Members of this clan are planners par excellence. They have an eye on the long term, and whether it is a business, shop, or online venture they take on, their persistence and organizational flair will ensure success. Commerce is their forte, and it doesn't take long for them to rise up the ranks to become head of department or CEO of the company.

Other than business, EIGHTS are also drawn to police work and to the legal profession, where their clever, agile minds coupled with their authoritative command add to the frisson of high court drama. Many are also drawn to politics, to managing sports clubs, or to running scientific laboratories.

Hardworking and restless, EIGHTS like to have many fingers in many pies, which is a means to their achievements. But this can also contribute to their losses. However, no matter how often EIGHTS take a tumble, financially or reputationally, they always manage to pick themselves up and sail on to even-greater glories than before.

The high-tech industries are especially rich grounds for these people's talents, who are drawn to start-up companies that they grow and then sell for a small fortune.

Financially, money is a big motivator to members of this group, who are economic whiz kids. They fear poverty, rarely gamble, save wisely, and put their cash into solid investments. Although not extravagant, when it comes to parting with money they nevertheless like to buy the best. With an eye for top quality, their purchases seem not only to last but also to increase in value.

DESTINY OR EXPRESSION
NUMBER NINE AT WORK

People belonging to this group are blessed with international flair. When working, mentally and physically NINES like to sweep with a broad brush, taking in the bigger picture and constantly looking to the farther horizon.

Paramount broadcasters, their ability to inspire others with their visions and stories naturally draws many NINES into the spoken and written media. They make fine television presenters, journalists, novelists, and playwrights.

Because there is something of the crusader in the makeup of the NINES, politics and the legal profession are two other career avenues that suit these people's humanitarian temperament. With their verbal skills and powers of persuasion, members of this group can become leading lights, wielding immense influence in the community in which they serve, righting wrongs being one of their strongest motivators.

For those of a more physically active disposition, the sports arena is another area in which NINES can excel. Others will choose to make a name for themselves in the entertainment industry, growing to be loved by their audiences and adored by their fans.

NINES toil long and hard for their fame and glory. Few can boast overnight success. In fact, whether through long hours of study or training, this group in general struggles on for many years before they reach the acclaim they deserve.

With colleagues, NINES are imaginative and encouraging. As employers, they have the persuasive knack of imbuing their staff with confidence. Because they themselves are ambitious and competitive, they respect—and expect—a similar drive among their employees.

Financially, although day-to-day expenses may sometimes be precarious with this group, especially in the early years of their careers, it is those big dreams and schemes of theirs that can eventually come up trumps, turning an apparently doomed venture into a roaring success. For NINES, money is a vehicle to freedom, allowing them the time and space not only to pursue their wider interests, but also to satisfy their natural instinct for generosity. Many benefactors are born into this group.

CHAPTER FIVE

KEY TO
THE DOOR

HAVE YOU NOTICED

how each house seems to have a specific character all its own? Some always feel friendly and welcoming, even on a dull, rainy day. Others have a stiff, clinical feel to them, cool and indifferent as you walk in, so you don't know whether to stand or sit. And when invited to "make yourself at home," you perch uncomfortably on the edge of an upright chair.

Some houses are chaotic, their owners never able to find what they're looking for. Some have an obviously artistic or high-brow feel to them. Some feel homely and cozy, while others feel positively unwelcoming—cold, dark, and brooding. There are those that each successive owner occupies for a good twenty or thirty years, growing and establishing a whole new generation in them, while an almost identical house in the same street might, for some seemingly inexplicable reason, change hands as often as every couple of years.

Certainly it is undeniable that houses will reflect their inhabitants, which will, of course, depend a great deal on the occupants' way of life, style, and taste, not to mention their pocket. Moreover, bricks and mortar, it has been suggested, are able to absorb the atmosphere that people create within their walls—happiness, sadness, avariciousness, malice—and these vibrations may be retained within that residence long, long after its occupants have moved away. These, of course, are the vibrations that sensitive prospective buyers or tenants are likely to pick up on the minute they enter through the front door.

And isn't it interesting to note how houses seem to attract similar types of people? Perhaps, it might be argued, that's something to do with income brackets—people within the same income level can afford the same type of house, or that the size or setting of the property favors a certain age group or stage in life of its prospective inhabitants. Possibly that is so, but according to numerology, there is more to it than that.

Indeed, there is a good deal more to the character of a house than the vagaries of its occupants, something that is hinted at when every so often one hears people bemoaning their fate: "Ever since we moved into this house, we've had nothing but trouble!" Or more positively, others might say, "Our new house has brought us luck; moving here was the best thing we ever did!"

Could there be such a thing, then, as a lucky or unlucky house? Or a happy/unhappy, friendly/hostile, warm/cold one? And could it be that people really do find a particular affinity to certain houses, feeling immediately comfortable and more at ease in some locations than in others?

A numerologist would say yes. The answer, they surmise, lies in the compatible vibrations between the house and its occupant. But to state categorically that one house is luckier than another is not quite correct. Each house, like each number, has its positive and negative sides. What matters, however, is that the vibratory influence of the house should match that of its inhabitant. If the two are in harmony, the individual will feel at peace and will flourish and even prosper. If there is an obvious clash, however, the individual may feel hindered, blocked, ill at ease, physically or psychologically stuck.

Determining the character of your house and what sort of vibration it is putting out is simply the process of analyzing its address, taking its street number, and adding up any multiples until reduced to a single digit. Whether that house is compatible with you, how it will influence your life and how you are likely to react while living there, will very much depend on your own date of birth, or Destiny Number. If the two numbers are in harmony with each other, you will probably feel a comfortable symbiosis with that house, a place that should prove beneficial to you and be somewhere where, in all probability, you feel you will thrive. Digits that are discordant, however, may explain why the occupant feels uncomfortable at that address, or even—in extreme cases—may help throw some light upon why their luck seems to have taken a downward turn.

The first step, then, is to analyze the actual number of your house. If you live in a house that's numbered 1 to 9, simply refer to that number in the table of houses below. If yours is a multiple—32, say, add the digits together: 3 + 2 = 5, then look up the description for the number 5. Larger numbers can be reduced in the same way, such as, for example, 296, which becomes 2 + 9 + 6 = 17; 1 + 7 = 8.

If you live in an apartment block, the number of the block itself must be added to your apartment number and reduced to a single digit in the same way.

Example
Apt. 9, 25 Acacia Avenue
9 + 2 + 5 = 16
Total 1 + 6 = 7

An apartment block presents a good deal of interest to a numerologist because the number on the door of an individual apartment may in itself be incompatible with the street number of the block. If there is a mismatch in the vibrations, it is possible that petty frustrations or irritations may dog the inhabitants unfortunate enough to reside there. Chances are this is the one apartment that has the fastest turnover of tenants, or where the heating system constantly needs attention, where the plumbing leaks, or where for some inexplicable reason there is a recurring malfunction with the internet connection—generally the apartment that gives the janitor the biggest headache!

Of course, some houses don't have a number at all but are known by a name. According to the UK's Royal Mail, "Rose Cottage" is about the most popular name for a house in Britain. To find the vibrational character of "Rose Cottage" or Buckingham Palace or the White House, simply work out the numerical equivalent of the letters, just as you would for a person's name.

Example 1

ROSE	COTTAGE
9+6+1+5	3+6+2+2+1+7+5
2 + 1 = 3	2 + 6 = 8
3 + 8 = 11	

Total   1 + 1 = 2

Example 2

BUCKINGHAM	PALACE
2+3+3+2+9+5+7+8+1+4	7+1+3+1+3+5
4 + 4 = 8	2 + 0 = 2
8 + 2 = 10	

Total   1 + 0 = 1

Example 3

THE	WHITE	HOUSE
2+8+5	5+8+9+2+5	8+6+3+1+5
1+5 = 6	2 + 9 = 11 = 2	2 + 3 = 5
6 + 2 + 5 = 13		

Total   1 + 3 = 4

So, first calculate the number of your residence and then match that to the day of your birth. If you were born on the 21st of the month, your vibrational number is 2 + 1 = 3. And of course it's also 3 if you were born on the 3rd, on the 12th, and on the 30th of the month too. Add that figure to the year of your birth, reducing down until you have a single digit. Then check that against your house number in the House-Personality Compatibility Table that follows. These vibrational influences apply specifically to a property, a residence, or your work address and should not be used for the purpose of personal compatibility between people.

Of course, this table of affinities is just a guide, and it should be remembered that each number has a positive as well as a negative side to it, so that the character of a house will not be all good or all bad. The important thing is to recognize and try to live up to the nature of the challenge of, first, your own Destiny and Expression Numbers and, second, to the nature and challenge presented by your environment as expressed by the number of the house in which you live.

If, having tried, you still feel at odds with the vibrational influence of your house, in that whatever you do you still feel unsettled, unhappy, blocked, uneasy, lacking enthusiasm, or whatever, you can take comfort in the fact that, numerically speaking, there is an easy way out. Short of putting your property on the market again, it is possible to change an unsuitable vibrational influence of a house into a more favorable one simply by changing its numerical value.

So if, for example, your Destiny Number is 7 and you're finding it tough living at a No. 15 (1 + 5 = 6), think about giving your house a name—the numerical value of which, of course, should equal a number compatible with your own.

Example

	THE	LAURELS
	2+8+5	3+1+3+9+5+3+1
	1 + 5 = 6	2 + 5 = 7
	6 + 7 = 13	
Total	1 + 3 = 4	

For a Destiny Number 7, then, "The Laurels," with a numerical value of 4, would be a most compatible house name.

What is the essential aura of your house, and how does it relate to your own vibration? Match your number in the House-Personality Compatibility Table and then discover the numerological significance of your address in "The Character Guide to Your Home" section that follows.

HOUSE-PERSONAL COMPATIBILITY TABLE

Birth Day Or Destiny Number	Compatible House Numbers	Discordant House Numbers
1st and all numbers reducing to ONE: 10th, 19th, 28th.	All numbers adding to: 1, 2, 4, 7.	All numbers adding to: 6.
2nd and all numbers reducing to TWO: 11th, 20th, 29th.	All numbers adding to: 2, 6, 8.	All numbers adding to: 5.
3rd and all numbers reducing to THREE: 12th, 21st, 30th.	All numbers adding to: 1, 3, 5, 6, 7, 9.	All numbers adding to: 4.
4th and all numbers reducing to FOUR: 13th, 22nd, 31st.	All numbers adding to: 2, 4, 7.	All numbers adding to: 3, 5, 9.
5th and all numbers reducing to FIVE: 14th, 23rd.	All numbers adding to: 1, 3, 5, 7, 8, 9.	All numbers adding to: 2, 4, 6.
6th and all numbers reducing to SIX: 15th, 24th.	All numbers adding to: 3, 6, 9.	All numbers adding to: 1, 5, 7, 8.
7th and all numbers reducing to SEVEN: 16th, 25th.	All numbers adding to: 1, 2, 4, 7.	All numbers adding to: 6, 8, 9.
8th and all numbers reducing to EIGHT: 17th, 26th.	All numbers adding to: 1, 3, 8.	All numbers adding to: 7.
9th and all numbers reducing to NINE: 18th, 27th.	All numbers adding to: 3, 6, 9.	All numbers adding to: 4, 7.

CHARACTER GUIDE TO YOUR HOUSE

HOUSE No. 1

No. 1 houses, and all those adding up to one, may be characterized as lively and dynamic. These are busy, bustling households, full of life and activity. In line with this general bustle, No. 1 homes very often have two entrances to the property, thus augmenting the comings and goings.

Because of the dominant and active nature of this number, occupants of No. 1 houses will be sporty and energetic. So in this home there will be lots of sports equipment lying around. With No. 1 there is also an association with creativity, a sense of originality, and because of this there is likely to be evidence throughout of creative projects that have been undertaken. As well as the physical movement here is also found plenty of mental activity, and its residents are likely to enjoy intellectual pursuits. Perhaps they play quizzes and word games, possibly they indulge in literary pleasures, and there are bound to be several computers and other tech equipment for the young masterminds in the family. Occupants of No. 1 love traveling, and, like all travelers, these people will return with armfuls of memories and souvenirs with which to adorn their nests, which will be constant reminders of their adventures—and of even-greater adventures in more-distant horizons as yet to be conquered and explored. All in all, No. 1 may be described as a fairly cosmopolitan house.

HOUSE No. 2

In contrast to the active nature of the No. 1 house, a No. 2 address has a far quieter and more passive feel. There is a definite aura of peacefulness here, and its inhabitants will strive to achieve domestic harmony and tranquility. Very often there is a predominantly feminine influence in a No. 2 residence, with evidence of heightened sensitivity all round.

Much attention will be given to detail, although this is often at the expense of the larger, more important, and sometimes structural maintenance jobs that need to be routinely carried out. As a consequence, there is a certain ambiguity about this house—on the one hand, there is a sense of deterioration; yet, on the other hand, there will be strong focal points dotted around everywhere, which have been lavished with a good deal of love and care.

And this ambiguity, this duality that is so much a part of the No. 2 nature, can filter through and have a profound effect on its inhabitants. People living here who are not in harmony with its vibrations may especially feel unable to settle, conflicted by complex life situations or issues of health.

Those who are in harmony with this number, however, will find living here conducive to contemplation, to the growth of deep, inner wisdom, and to the development of their spiritual or psychic potential.

HOUSE No. 3

The No. 3 house is characterized by its carefree, easygoing atmosphere. Look around, and everywhere will be found evidence of a love and appreciation of creativity and art. This home will be filled with many original touches, furnished with flair and decorated with a strong sense of imagination and individuality.

Occupants of No. 3 houses are noted for their wide diversity of interests. New subjects, new ideas, new inventions, and new hobbies are a constant source of fascination, and half-finished projects will be evident throughout the house—started with great excitement and then left in midair as the enthusiasm has waned.

Activity is a keyword to this lively and colorful home, which sees a constant stream of visitors through its doors. This is a place of mental expansion, of learning and developing one's talents. If the occupants are prepared to take on this challenge, to make full use of their creative instincts, their artistic talents, and their inspirational ideas, they will be rewarded with fulfillment and success.

Indeed, for those who are in harmony with its vibrations, this is a place of happiness and good cheer. There will not be a serious sense of want, even if perhaps money is at times a little tight, because THREE is the number of abundance and good fortune.

But those whose personal number does not resonate harmoniously with THREE, who take a more methodical and down-to-earth approach to life, may find that residing here may not be altogether supportive of their needs.

HOUSE No. 4

No. 4 is a solid, reliable, hardworking type of household. An air of stability pervades, and throughout there is a feeling of orderliness, organization, and regularity.

Here, conservative and traditional values are maintained. Set roles are likely to be the order of the day, with a strong adherence to rules and regulations. The work ethic is nowhere more evident than at this address, where discipline and application go hand in hand with duty and responsibility.

Routine is important to the occupants here, who, in general, are not considered terribly versatile or, indeed, great lovers of change. In fact, they succeed by dint of constant perseverance at a task, stolidly plodding their way through to its completion.

There may not be a conspicuous amount of money in this house for paying professional experts to carry out building or installation jobs so the onus is likely to fall upon its inhabitants to do the work themselves. Fortunately, occupants of No. 4 are hardworking and willingly have a go at projects whether they have the requisite skills or not.

HOUSE No. 5

A No. 5 address is typified by lots of comings and goings. Perhaps it is best described as a typical bachelor pad, a pied-à-terre rather than a traditional family home. Somewhere to pass through, perhaps, but because of its lack of a stable sense of permanence, it does not necessarily inspire you to see it as a place in which to put down long-term roots.

Generally colorful and bright, this is, in many instances, a showy type of residence, keeping itself tidy by virtue of the fact that its inhabitants are often away. There is a restless feel to this house, and strangely enough, No. 5 seems to attract those who tend to be on the move a great deal—sales people, perhaps, frequent fliers or those in the media whose work requires them to travel extensively.

That same restlessness means that its occupants dislike routine just as much in their home as in their work. Consequently, they like to experiment with different color schemes, move the furniture around, or swap items from one room to another, so that you may visit this house one week and—upon returning the next—find yourself in such unfamiliar surroundings that you think you've gone to the wrong address altogether.

Light and space are often features of this house, created by lots of picture windows and an open-plan effect. But always there is a sensual character to No. 5: rich wines and sweetmeats to interest the palate; deep, inviting sofas in which to lose oneself; and mirrors everywhere to further reflect the light.

As well as sensuality, there is often an accompanying avant-garde or progressive element, with technological equipment and gadgets of all descriptions lying around, reflecting the love of communications that is so much a part not only of the residents but also of the general mercurial nature that describes the No. 5 dwelling. It is because of this mercurial character that No. 5s, and any other addresses that reduce to a FIVE, do so well as commercial premises, cottage industries, or residences with a dedicated home office.

HOUSE No. 6

Synonymous with domesticity and family life, the No. 6 abode characterizes the home.

Nowhere on the street is the sense of family unity, of domestic togetherness, of hearth and home more in evidence than at this house. Anyone walking in through the door can immediately sense the warm and homely atmosphere and get a feel of the lively, lived-in place filled with light, noise, laughter, and the bustle everywhere of domestic activity.

Children are at the heart of this home, their toys scattered around, their pictures displayed on the walls, their pets curled up in front of the fire.

Here will be found a blend of the practical with the creative so that there will be evidence of many artistic or handicraft projects everywhere. Perhaps cloths that have been prettily hand-embroidered will be draped over tables; lovingly stitched tapestries hang on the walls, adding color to the room; furniture bought for a song and cleverly restored takes pride of place; and tastefully arranged flowers picked from the garden are a testament to its green-thumbed occupants.

The No. 6 house encapsulates all that is creative, the love and nurturing of children and family, the spirit of beauty and harmony, and the very heart of home.

HOUSE No. 7

There is something cool and cerebral about the No. 7 house. Even its occupants, people who—preferring to keep themselves to themselves and thus considered aloof—seem to create an air of secrecy and mystery about them. Since they tend not to be the most social of people, it is often the case that neighbors barely know who they are at all. Perhaps one reason for this is that, apart from No. 5, there seems to be a faster turnover of residents at this address than at any other in the area.

From the outside, No. 7 houses can appear somewhat neglected. There can be a look of faded glory about them, a sense of past grandeur now slightly tired. And yet, coupled to that is an implicit feeling that in the right hands, their former elegance and beauty can readily be restored.

Inside, the same sense of elegance, albeit in decline, is also in evidence throughout, matched by obvious attempts at creating a certain stylish interior—although all too often, this is achieved at the expense of comfort. Don't expect to find any unnecessary frills or furbelows here. Quality rather than quantity being the way of the No. 7 home, this house is often sparsely furnished or goes for the minimalist look, which altogether adds to its feel of cool detachment.

No. 7 houses generate a quiet and peaceful atmosphere that is conducive to work of an intellectual nature, to study, or to inner contemplation rather than to the noisy traffic and hurley-burley of family life. They do especially well as churches, libraries, or academic institutions.

HOUSE No. 8

The No. 8 house is associated with material security, plenty, and success, and thus this number on the door, or those adding up to an EIGHT, will reflect an air of prosperity.

The prevailing atmosphere is that of material comfort. Its inhabitants are invariably ambitious, industrious, and successful in their work. Often, they are business people and achievement motivated, so they are prepared to work long hours in order to climb the ladder and arrive at their goal. And their efforts are certainly rewarded in material terms.

The long hours that residents of this number put into their jobs or professions mean that they are out a lot during the day and thus not available to do many of the everyday, routine domestic tasks that are essential to the maintenance and good running of a house. But since they earn a good salary due to all their hard work, they can afford the latest technological labor-saving devices and staff to help them run their day-to-day affairs.

As a result, there is a feeling of affluence around this house: conspicuous consumption, material comforts, and gadgets much in evidence. But what may also be apparent is that the occupants of No. 8 are so busy acquiring wealth and amassing possessions that often there is little time left to enjoy the true warmth of family life.

Residents whose personal number resonates harmoniously with No. 8 and who are prepared to work hard to achieve material stability together with emotional fulfillment will be well rewarded during their stay in this house. Those, however, who do not feel an affinity toward this address or who are unable to meet these challenges could well experience hindrances here.

HOUSE No. 9

This is a very busy place! Expect masses of activity here, with a constant stream of people passing through. Yet, though there may be lots of irons in the fire, underlying it all will be a general feeling that not a lot is accomplished, and progress in any direction is slow.

Residents of No. 9 houses, or those adding up to 9, are full of ambitions and good ideas, forever making plans for the future. A good deal of this, however, may be put down to pure daydreaming, because these good intentions are all too often left on the drawing board or hanging in midair. The ideas are certainly there, but the practical application or implementation of them can all too often be lacking in this household.

One of the biggest problems in this respect is that money can be a bit tight, and there simply isn't enough to cover all those essential little household tasks, let alone stretch to achieving all the dreams and longings of its inhabitants. Sometimes the difficulties lie in the fact that No. 9 occupants are more idealistic than materialistic and simply don't go in for highly paid occupations. Alternatively, the fact that many are neither practical nor materialistic may suggest that they are unable to manage their finances successfully.

Often for them, hopes and dreams are left to bubble away on a back burner until such time when, with family financial demands diminishing, they find time and opportunity to follow and fulfill their long-dreamed-after ambitions.

The prevailing atmosphere in the No. 9 household is one of creativity with, for many, a somewhat cosmopolitan feel. Since NINE symbolizes a global outlook, this house is likely to have a good aspect, with plenty of windows that let in light and allow its inhabitants a good vantage point from which to observe the world around them, to contemplate philosophy and the universal truths of life.

CONCLUSION: A WORLD OF WONDER

So far, the *Magic of Numbers* has traveled through the fascinating meanings of the primary digits 1 to 9. They are the first steps taking us through the basic knowledge that opens the door to a new world of wonder. From this threshold we can see far into the distance, along roads that twist and turn through octaves and resonances, that intersect with Super Numbers, that spin us through cycles and give us a glimpse into the future.

Numbers lead us through days of the month: When is the best day to move house, to set off on vacation, to pitch your idea to the boss, to get married? Numbers reveal our lucky years: when to apply for that great job, when you're likely to meet "The One," when an ambition has the best chance of coming to fruition. And numbers also help us recognize when we need to exert caution, when our energies are down, and when we just need to sit still and observe.

Understanding numbers opens our awareness, shows us the interconnections that govern our lives, and gives us the knowledge we need to control our destinies.

These are the next steps. And the journey has only just begun.

ABOUT THE AUTHOR

Lori Reid is a bestselling author and one of the UK's top astrologers and hand analysts. She has written more than 50 books, which have been translated into over 30 languages. Her features have appeared nationally and internationally in *OK!, Marie Claire, Biteki* magazines, and others. She has made several appearances on TV, including BBC1, GMTV, and UK Living. For many years she wrote the astrological forecasts for *The Daily* and *Sunday Express*. She is the author of *Your Health in Your Hands* (REDFeather) and lives in the UK. http://lorireid.co.uk